inventions

HOW?

HOW DOES THE KEYBOARD PUT WORDS ON THE SCREEN?

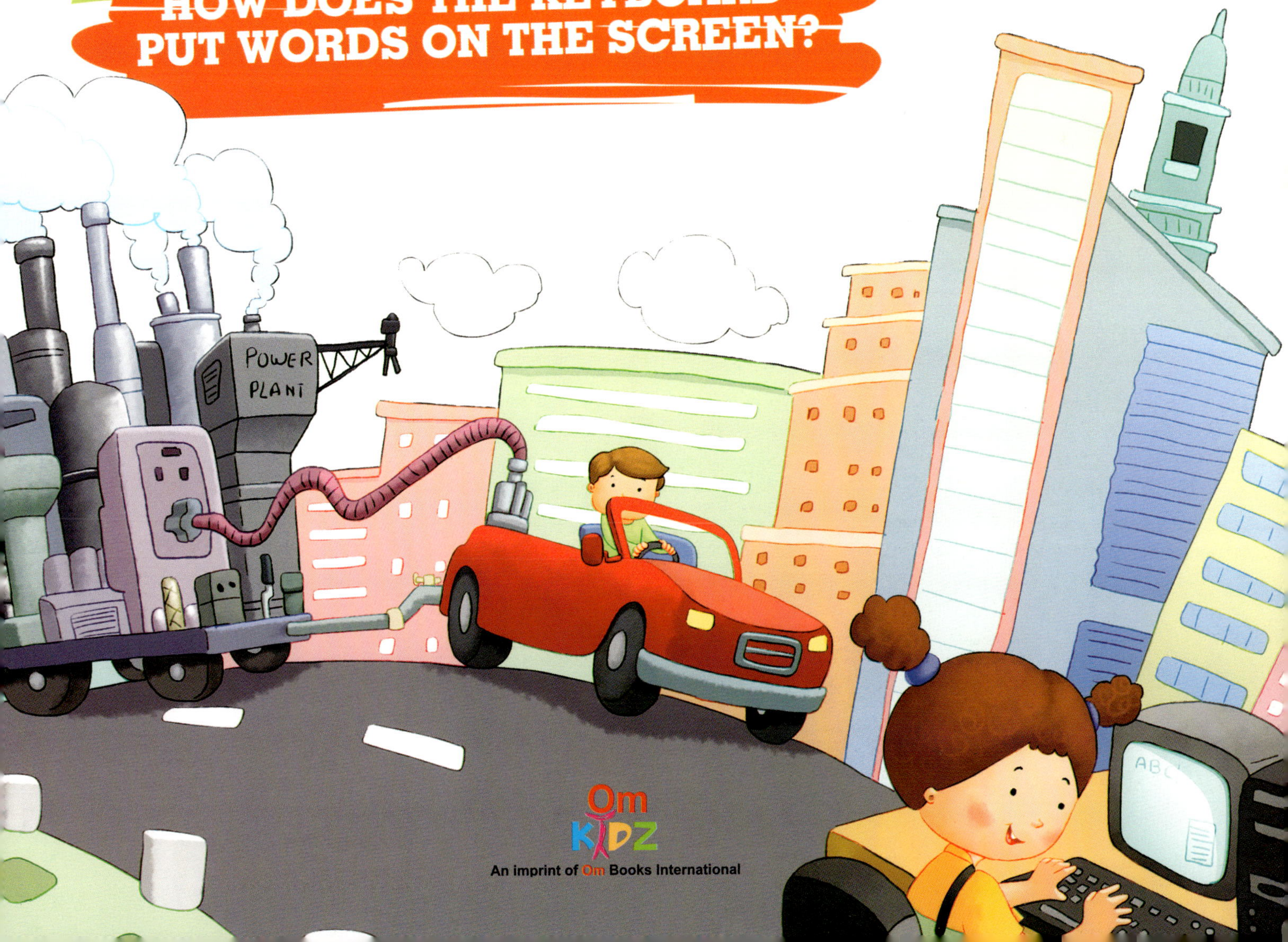

Om KIDZ
An imprint of Om Books International

HOW?

CONTENTS

1 How old is the oldest invention?

It's as old as 3.3 million years! The oldest inventions are said to be the most basic stone implements that were made by early humans. These include stone cores, hammerstones, anvils and sharp stone flakes. These tools were made by hitting stones against each other, or applying pressure with wood or bones. Early men used these tools for hunting and protecting themselves.

Pocket fact

The world's oldest stone tools were discovered from the shores of Lake Turkana in Kenya, and are almost 3.3 million years old!

2 How was fire discovered?

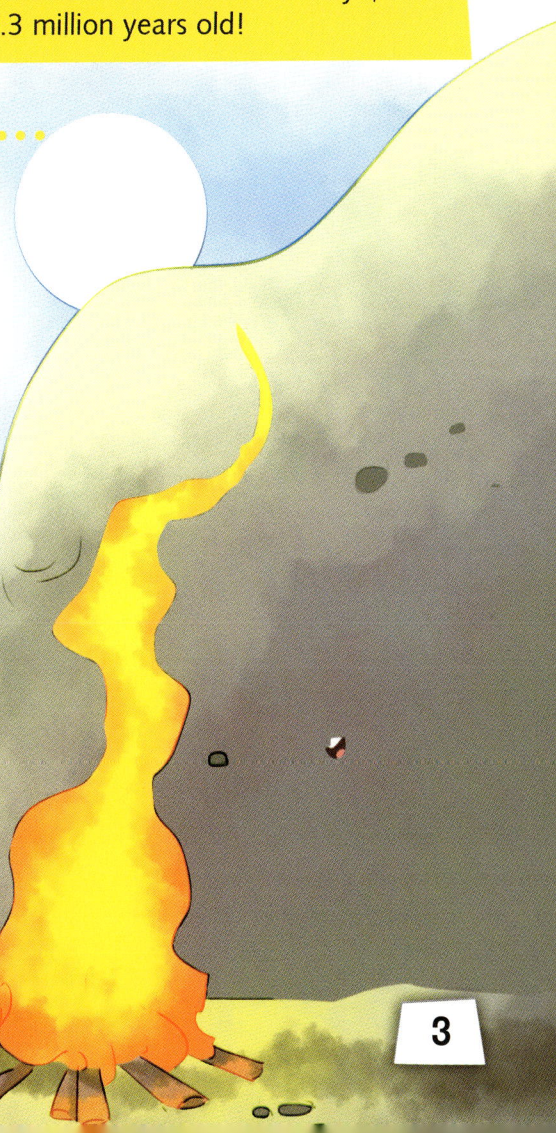

There are several theories about how fire was discovered. Some believe that pre-humans first noticed fire after lightning struck a tree. It is said that then they must have learned to make fire using sticks and flint. Soon, they discovered that it was possible to use fire for heat and light, and also for cooking food.

Find out!

How did the ancient Greeks light a fire?

Find out!

Name the parts of a wheel.

3 How were wheels used in ancient times?

They first served as a potter's wheel! Wheels first appeared in Mesopotamia around 5,000 years ago. They were initially used by potters for shaping clay. It was much later that wheels were fitted to carts, which made movement much easier.

Pocket fact

Throughout history, most inventions were inspired by the natural world. The idea to invent fork came from forked sticks; the airplane from gliding birds. But the wheel was not inspired by any existing object; it was purely man's innovation.

4 How does the modern wheel work?

A piece of wood called crossbar runs from one side of the wheel to the other to make it stronger. These are spokes that link the middle of the wheel to the outer edge to enable the wheels to function properly.

5 How old are the first written records?

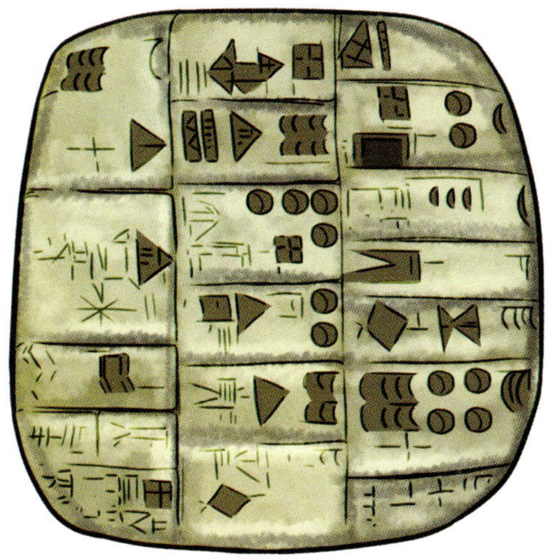

Approximately 5,000 years old! The earliest writing we know of dates back to around 3000 BCE and was probably invented by the Sumerians, who lived in southern Mesopotamia. However, it was very different from present-day writing. Most early writing systems began with symbols and small images instead of words.

Pocket fact

The quill, the hollow shaft of a bird's feather, was also used as a writing tool in the ancient times. It was first used as a pen in around 500 CE.

6 How did the first writing tool look like?

It was a pointed tool! The Sumerians are credited with the invention of the first writing tool called a 'stylus'. It was made from reed, a strong thin plant, and produced a wedge shape each time it was pressed into wet clay.

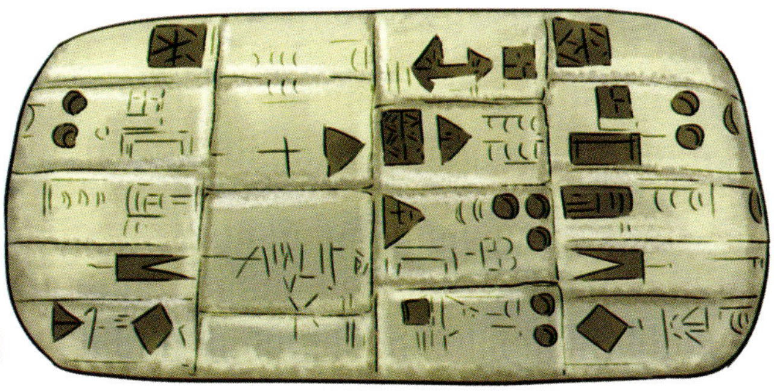

Find out!

Where did the alphabet first originate?

Find out!

What has the word 'paper' been derived from?

7 How was ink made in ancient times?

It was made of carbon! The first writing ink was invented by the Egyptians and the Chinese in 2500 BCE. It was made of carbon mixed with a solution of glue, or gum, and moulded into sticks. The sticks were dried, but were mixed with water before use.

Pocket fact

Johannes Gutenberg invented a special oil-based ink in the 1400s. This ink prevented blurry edges and worked well for Gutenberg's newly invented printing press.

8 How was paper first made?

It was made from mulberry bark! Papermaking dates back to about 105 CE, when Ts'ai Lun, an official attached to the imperial court of China made a sheet of paper using mulberry fibres. He made it by mixing mulberry bark and other fibres with old rags, hemp waste and fishnets. He then mashed it flat, pressed out the water and let it dry in the sun.

Find out!

Calculate 1010010 + 1001011 with the help of a calculator. Which number did you get?

9 How were calculations done in ancient times?

It started with fingers and other objects! The first method of calculation was to count on fingers. This gradually changed to the use of tallies that were made by carving notches in wood, bone and stone. Much later, around 1387 CE, the first calculating tool called the 'abacus' was used in Europe, China and Russia.

Pocket fact

The Chinese abacus called the 'Suanpan' had two beads on the rods on the upper side and five beads on the rods on the lower side of the divider. The upper beads are called the heaven beads, and the lower beads are called the earth beads.

10 How was the first mechanical calculator invented?

It was invented using metal wheel dials. The first mechanical calculator was invented in 1642 by Blaise Pascal. It had a polished brass box, about 350 mm x 125 mm x 75 mm in dimension. There were eight movable metal dials with the numbers zero to nine that were turned to the appropriate numbers using a stylus. The answers were displayed in boxes on the top of the calculator.

11 How were long-distance messages sent before the invention of telephones?

They were sent by telegraphs! The telegraph was first invented in 1791 by Claude and Rene Chappe in France. But it wasn't very successful. Later, in 1837, Samuel Morse developed the electric telegraph that worked by transmitting electrical signals over a wire laid between stations.

Pocket fact

The first-ever message over the telegraph was sent on 24 May 1844 by Morse. It was a passage from the Bible's Book of Numbers, and read 'What hath God wrought!'

12 How did the box telephone work?

The box telephone was invented by Alexander Graham Bell in 1876–1877. It was made of a wooden frame that had two electromagnets, wire terminals, a horseshoe magnet and a trumpet-shaped receiver. The receiver worked as both a mouthpiece and an earpiece. When someone spoke into the mouthpiece, it made the electromagnets vibrate. These vibrations turned into electric signals, which were sent to another telephone by wires attached to the two terminals.

Find out!

What did Graham Bell say to his assistant when he made the first phone call?

HOW?

Find out!

How fast can electricity travel?

13 How was electricity discovered?

It is said to have been discovered in 1752 by Benjamin Franklin. He conducted an experiment in order to show that lightning was electricity. He tied a metal key to a kite string and flew it during a thunderstorm to conduct electricity. Electricity from the storm clouds transferred to the metal key and flowed down the string!

Pocket fact

The first power plant, Pearl Street Power Station, built by Thomas Edison, became operative in the year 1882.

14 How did the first electric light look like?

It looked quite similar to a lantern! The first electric light was made in 1800 by an English scientist Humphry Davy. He attached a charcoal strip between the ends of two wires and connected the other ends of the wires to a battery. This charged the charcoal strip and made the carbon glow. Thus, the first arc lamp was invented.

15 How did the first trains look like?

They were like present-day wagons! Railways existed long before the invention of steam engine. They were used in European mines to move heavy wagonloads of coal along tunnels. The wagons first ran on parallel wooden planks, and then on iron rails. They were pulled by horses or people.

Pocket fact

In Japan, any train delays over five minutes, usually incurs an apology and a 'delay certificate' for the passengers on their way to work.

16 How was the first airplane different from the modern one?

It had many differences! The first airplane was invented by the Wright brothers in 1903. It was made of wood or canvas material and had warped light-weight wings. Its elevators were located on the front of the aircraft. On the other hand, modern airplanes are made of aluminium. They have ailerons on their wings to control the roll of the aircraft. Their elevators are located at the tail-end of the aircraft. Modern airplanes have a cockpit with high technological controls that the first airplane lacked.

Find out!

At what altitude does an airplane fly?

17 How did the early televisions work?

They displayed only black and white pictures! The first television was invented by Scottish inventor, John Logie Baird. Later a Russian-American inventor Vladimir Zworykin used the cathode-ray tube (a device used to show images on a screen) in a new type of electrical television. Early televisions had huge boxes and much smaller screens.

Pocket fact

The word 'television' was introduced in the English language in 1907. It was coined by the Russian scientist, Constantin Perskyi.

18 How are LED televisions different from cathode-ray tube ones?

They used LEDs to display images! LED televisions have small LEDs behind the screen that produce high-quality images with vibrant colours. Due to the use of LEDs, the screen is power efficient and much slimmer in size. On the other hand, cathode-ray tube TVs have a cathode-ray tube that displays the image on the screen. They are large in size and have wide viewing angles.

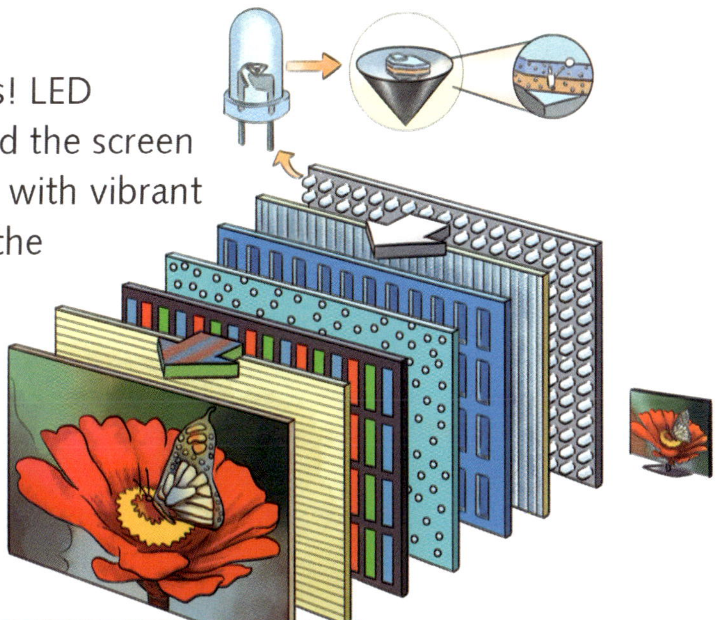

Find out!

What is the full form of LED?

Find out!

Compare the keys of a typewriter and a keyboard. List the differences.

19 How did the first computer look like?

It was huge and complicated! The Analytical Engine is generally considered as the first computer. It was invented by Charles Babbage in the early 19th century. It had four main parts that are the essential components of every computer today. The mill was the calculating unit (CPU in a modern computer), the store was where data was held prior to processing (memory in a modern computer), and the reader and printer were the input and output devices.

Pocket fact

The first electronic computer was called the ENIAC. It weighed more than 27 tons and measured 1800 square feet.

20 How was the first typewriter different from the modern one?

The first typewriter called the Sholes & Glidden was invented by Christopher Latham Sholes. This typewriter typed only in capital letters. Its keyboard was designed to separate frequently used pairs of type-bars so that they would not clash and get stuck at the printing point. It was a decorative machine with painted flowers and decals, and looked much like a sewing machine!

21 How did the idea of a QWERTY keyboard evolve?

It was invented due to the keys getting jammed! The QWERTY arrangement was designed in 1868 by Christopher Sholes, the inventor of the typewriter. The first keyboard had keys arranged in an alphabetical order, but people typed so fast that the keys got jammed. To solve this, the keys were randomly positioned to slow down the typing speed and prevent key jams.

Pocket fact

The longest key on every keyboard is the space bar. But in Japan, the statistical space bar is much shorter than anywhere else in the world.

22 How does the keyboard put words on the screen?

It works with the help of mechanical switches! The keyboard contains its own internal processor that receives electrical signals through keystrokes. Each key has a special-shaped arrangement at the bottom, known as the plunger. When you press a key, an electrical signal is sent to the keyboard's internal processor. The key which is pressed is detected and the letter gets typed on the screen!

Find out!

What is the use of the pause key on the keyboard?

Find out!

What is the length of a space shuttle?

23 How did the first telescope look like?

The first telescope was invented in 1608 by a Dutch spectacle-maker Hans Lippershey. He fitted two small lenses in a long tube. This is how the first telescope was made. In 1609, Galileo Galilei improved this telescope. Galileo's telescope was about 47-inches-long and had an objective diameter of two inches. It had an eyepiece that provided an upright image.

Pocket fact

The word telescope was derived from the Greek words 'tele' and 'scope' meaning 'far' and 'to look and see'.

24 How did the first space shuttle launch and land?

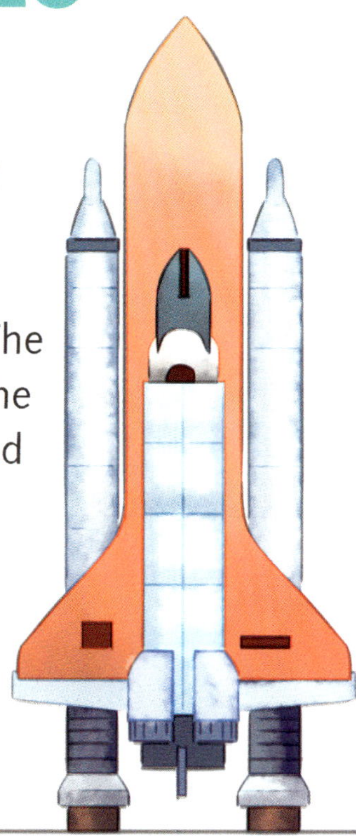

It launched like a rocket, but landed like a glider airplane! The space shuttle was launched by NASA. It had solid rocket boosters and main engines (on the orbiter), that helped the shuttle blast off from the Earth like a rocket. The two boosters dropped off the shuttle two minutes after the launch and fell into the ocean. The shuttle orbiter returned to Earth like an airplane, with wheels coming out from underneath its orbiter. It rolled to a stop on a runway.

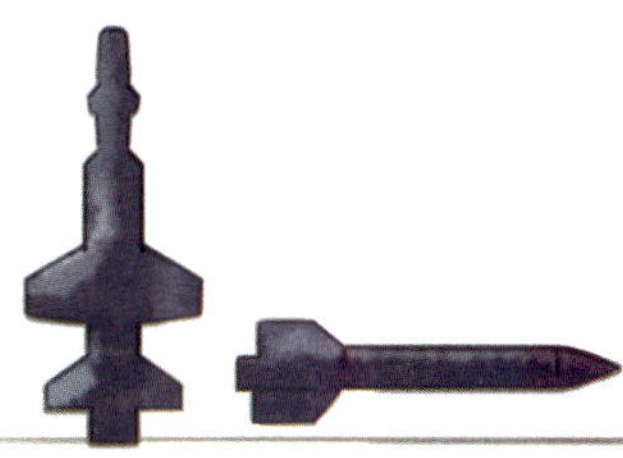

HOW?

Find out!

What was GPS earlier called?

25 How did the compass come into being?

The compass was invented by the Chinese. Chinese fortune tellers used a mineral called lodestone to construct their fortune-telling boards. The mineral consisted of an iron oxide, which aligns itself in a north–south direction. Eventually, it was noticed that the lodestones pointed out real directions. This led to the creation of the first compass. It was made on a square slab with a spoon-shaped device that would always point south.

Pocket fact

The first 'needle' of an iron needle compass was invented in China. It was shaped like a tadpole.

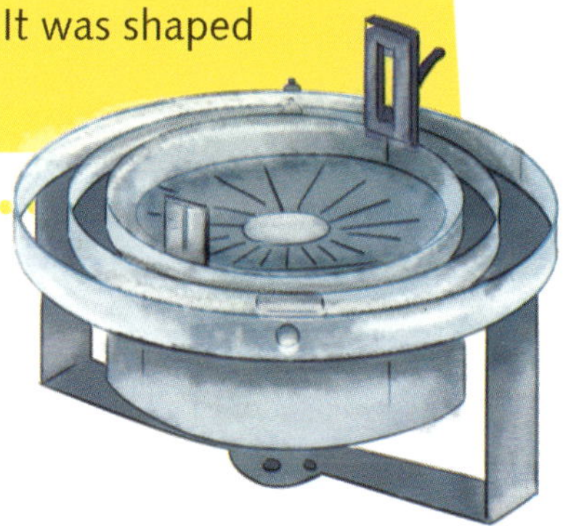

26 How old is the GPS system?

It started in 1957! The idea of GPS started with the satellite Sputnik. The US scientists working at Massachusetts Institute of Technology noticed that the frequency of the radio signals transmitted by the Russian satellite Sputnik increased as it approached, and decreased as it moved away. This gave them the idea to track satellites from the ground by measuring the frequency of the radio signals they emitted. And that, this could also be used to track the location of receivers on the ground from the satellites.

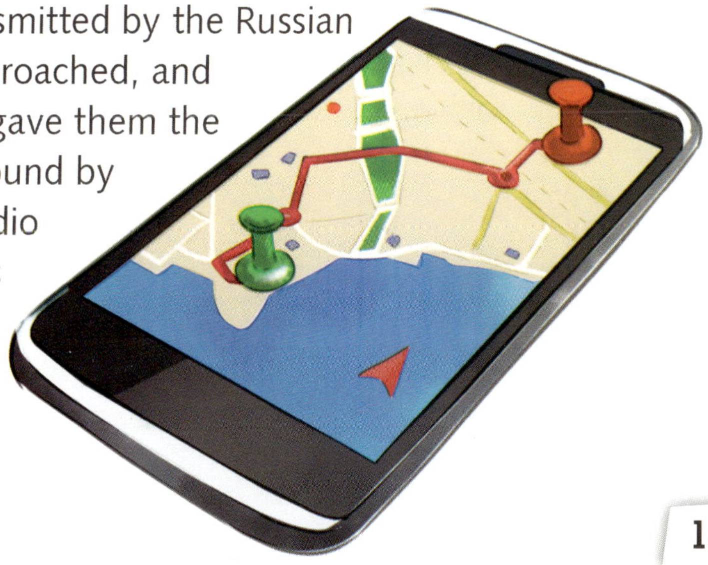

OTHER TITLES IN THIS SERIES